*Whoever controls the king,
controls the kingdom.*

HOLLY BLACK, *The Cruel Prince*

Willie, Willie, Harry, Steve,
Harry...

EMPRESS MATILDA

MY STORY

*as written by Sally Mortimore
and illustrated by Sally Castle*

Introduction by Lindy Grant

First published in the UK in 2025 by Two Rivers Press
7 Denmark Road, Reading RG1 5PA
www.tworiverspress.com

General Product Safety Regulations (GPSR) documentation:
www.tworiverspress.com/about/gpsr

EU GPSR Authorised Representative:
Logos Europe Ltd
9 Rue Nicolas Poussin, 17000 La Rochelle, France
contact@logoseurope.eu

ISBN 978-1-915048-28-8

1 2 3 4 5 6 7 8 9

Two Rivers Press is represented in the UK by Inpress Ltd
and distributed by BookSource, Glasgow.

Cover design and illustrations by Sally Castle
Text design by Sally Castle and Nadja Robinson and typeset
in Golden Cockerel.

Printed and bound in Great Britain by Halstan & Co., Amersham

Introduction

The Empress Matilda was indomitable and formidable. She was still a child when she was sent away by her parents, King Henry I of England and Queen Matilda, from her home in England, to marry Henry V, Emperor of Germany. As Henry's wife, she played an important role in governing his extensive lands, for he could not be everywhere in his vast domains at once.

But they had no children, and when Henry V died in 1125, Matilda returned to her father, who married her off to Count Geoffrey of Anjou.

It was not a happy marriage. Geoffrey was almost ten years younger than Matilda, and only a count. Matilda never forgot that she had been an empress: that was how she saw herself and how those around her referred to her.

Matilda had no surviving brother, and her father, Henry I, did his best to ensure that she would succeed him to the English throne. Women were not forbidden from ruling, but the great barons and churchmen expected that their ruler would be a man.

When Henry I died, Matilda's cousin Stephen of Blois seized the English throne. Matilda fought back with determination and courage, but Stephen managed to cling on to the crown.

Eventually, it was agreed that Matilda's son would become king of England after Stephen's death – which he did in 1154 as King Henry II. Henry was a strong ruler, who dominated the kingdom in a way Stephen had not.

Contemporaries believed that Henry learnt to rule so firmly from his mother the Empress, who taught

him how to keep those around him dependent
on his favour just as a falconer would train
a falcon.

Henry depended on Matilda to govern Normandy
for him, while he concentrated on his other lands –
England, Anjou and Aquitaine. Matilda was perhaps
more admired than loved.

When she died in 1167, she was buried in the abbey
of Le Bec in Normandy, to which she had given rich
gifts of golden religious objects. Her tomb there
defined her in terms of the men in her life:

> *Great by birth, greater by marriage,*
> *greatest in her offspring,*
> *here lies the daughter, wife and mother of Henry.*

It was a man's world.

Lindy Grant FSA, FRHistS
Professor Emeritus of Medieval History, University of Reading
Honorary Research Fellow, Courtauld Institute of Art

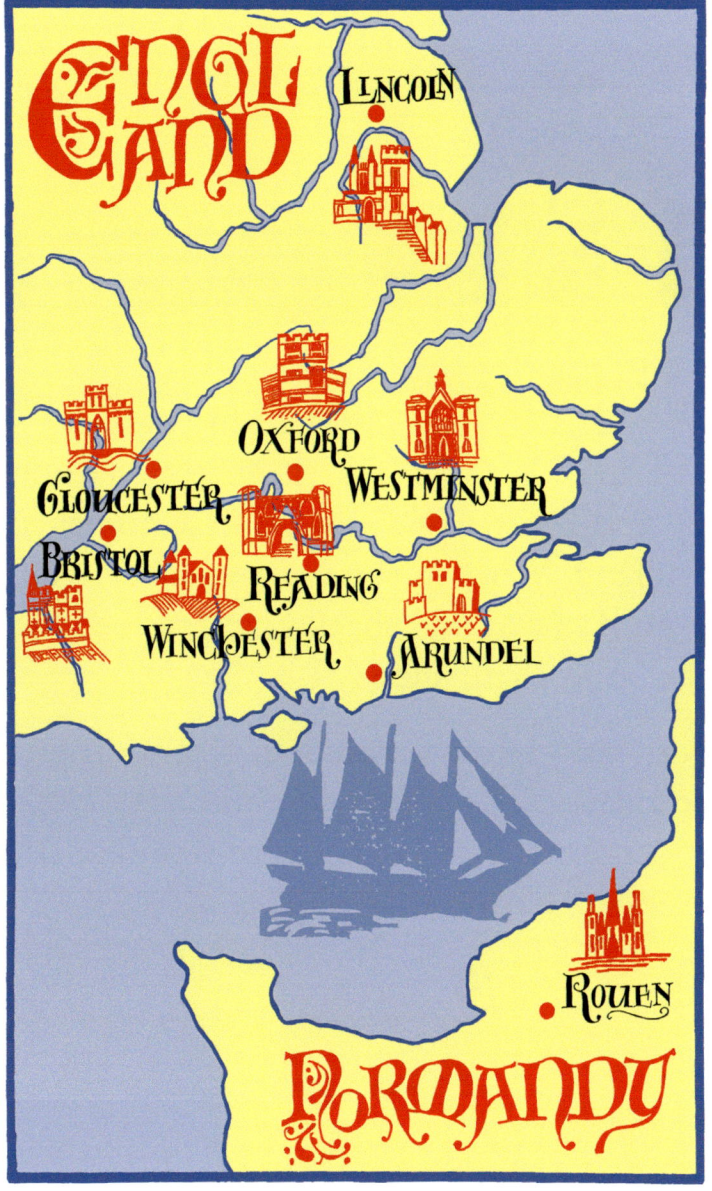

ENGLAND

LINCOLN

OXFORD

GLOUCESTER

WESTMINSTER

BRISTOL

READING

WINCHESTER

ARUNDEL

ROUEN

NORMANDY

reetings! I am Matilda — you may know me as Empress Matilda — and I was so nearly the first queen of England. William the Conqueror was my grandfather, and I should have succeeded my father, King Henry I.

For many years I ruled in the southern counties of England and came very close to seizing the crown back from my cousin, Stephen. However, it was not to be.

This is my story.

I am Matilda. This is my story.

I am known as Empress Matilda to distinguish me from all the other Matildas — it was a popular name. My mother's real name was Edith, but they called her Good Queen Maud, or Matilda of Scotland. Her father was King Malcolm III of Scotland and her mother, Margaret, was descended from Alfred the Great, the famed Anglo-Saxon King. So I'm the great, great, great... granddaughter of a great king. But I digress. I was talking about Matildas: there's me, my mother and my cousin — Matilda of Boulogne (more about her later). My grandmother was Matilda of Flanders and there was also Matilda of Savoy, queen of Portugal.

here's a reason we were all called Matilda. It means 'Mighty in Battle' and we were. Battles aren't just fought with swords, you know. My weapons were a talent for strategy, a head for planning and organisation, and a heart for justice. Justice is my driving force, the motivation for all my actions and the key to my story. It's said that my Scottish grandmother, St Margaret, was the real power behind King Malcolm — she taught him and all her children to be just and holy rulers.

eanwhile, my French grandmother, Matilda of Flanders, funded William's invasion in 1066 and co-ruled England after the Conquest, developing a reputation as a wise judge. And my mother didn't leave the government to her husband, King Henry I, but took care of things in England when my father was away in Normandy, looking after the affairs of government and organising building projects. Did you know, she built London's first public toilets at Queenhithe? And two hospitals.

My mother built the first public toilets.

I was betrothed to Henry V, king of Germany, when I was 8 years old. It may seem young to you, but I was ready for it. My upbringing and education had prepared me. I knew my destiny was to rule. Marrying me would create a powerful alliance between Germany and the Anglo-Norman kingship — remember my father was duke of Normandy as well as king of England. I was crowned queen of Germany on 25 July 1110 — the start of my 'secondary' education on German culture and manners. And life started to get very interesting... The very next year, my future husband captured the Pope!

My future husband captured the Pope!
He imprisoned him in St Peter's Basilica

he reasons are complex, but he imprisoned the Pope in St Peter's Basilica in Rome until he agreed to crown Henry as Holy Roman Emperor — the most powerful monarch in Europe. He was helped by yet another Matilda, Matilda of Tuscany — an extremely rich and powerful ally. Henry came home to Germany, and we were married in 1114 when I was 12.

owever, Henry had made a powerful enemy in the Church. He was excommunicated by the Archbishop of Vienne and his ally, Matilda of Tuscany, died. My chance to get properly involved in politics had arrived! Henry and I marched over the Alps in 1116 to take control of northern Italy and advance on Rome itself. Our expedition was more successful than we'd anticipated. The Pope fled, leaving us in charge. When Henry had to return to Germany, I stayed and presided over court, acting as Henry's regent and commanding the Imperial Army. That was my first taste of government, and I liked it.

Henry and I marched over the Alps
in 1116 to take control of northern Italy
and advance on Rome.

But disaster struck. My mother died in 1118. She had been my mentor and confidante, someone whose advice I trusted more than my husband's or even my father's. She understood people and how to work with them to make things happen. She didn't need to command, threaten or wheedle. Instead, she used reason and logic and a strong sense of what was right. I missed her terribly.

And before I had got over her death, a catastrophic shipwreck killed my brother, William. I say catastrophic because as well as William's, it took the life of all his friends. The White Ship struck the rock they call Quilleboeuf and sank, but no one could understand quite why it happened. That route from Normandy to England was well-travelled; my father and his advisers (and some enemies) were always sailing back and forth between their power bases. Rumours surfaced of heavy drinking and a party on board. Three hundred people were on that ship and there was one survivor, a butcher from Rouen called Berold, who managed to cling to the rock.

There was one survivor, a butcher from Rouen
called Berold.

L say one survivor, but there were in fact two. Stephen of Blois, my cousin on my father's side, had boarded the ship at the same time as William but disembarked before it sailed because he wasn't feeling well. Stephen's survival was to have a dramatic impact on my life and prospects.

hey say bad luck comes in threes and a few years later in 1125, my husband, Henry V, died. He was 20 years older than me, and we had no children so there was no obvious successor on his death. History looks unfavourably on Henry as a traitor, betraying his own father, and as an oppressor of the Church. They even blamed our childlessness on his sins. But the line a king treads between opposing factions is a fine one and, while he made mistakes (imprisoning a Pope is never ideal), he was motivated by an underlying desire for unification of the Empire.

So, at the age of 23, the losses of my mother, brother and husband were further compounded by the loss of my title, my home and my lands. I returned to Normandy with just my jewels, two of Henry's crowns and a treasured sacred relic — the hand of St James the Apostle. This was presented to Reading Abbey and among many miracles, it healed a woman from Earley of dropsy, while Edward Haver of Reading was cured of a tumour.

I returned to Normandy with just
my jewels, two of Henry's crowns
and a treasured sacred relic.

STEPHEN OF · BLOIS ♥   MATILDA · OF BOULOGNE ♥

My cousin married Matilda of Boulogne

y father married again, and I slowly became more and more involved in his court. With no (legitimate) male heirs, there were continuous rumblings about succession and I was frustrated by my father's indecisiveness. No one had any doubt about my competence to rule; I had more experience than most of the candidates, even at my young age. But my cousin, Stephen of Blois — the one who had survived the White Ship disaster — was also in the frame. His sizeable power base in England was further strengthened by marriage to my cousin on my mother's side — the wealthy Matilda of Boulogne.

atilda was to be my nemesis. She became queen of England while I did not. We were not enemies. We'd had the same upbringing. The same principles of just and holy rule were passed down to both of us from our Scottish grandmother, along with our talents for governing, negotiating and getting things done.

But let's rewind because at first, I had the upper hand. My father finally named me as his successor. The barons were gathered in Westminster at Christmas 1126, and in a ceremony in January, they swore allegiance to me. My power base was enhanced through a strategic but unhappy marriage to Geoffrey of Anjou — more than 10 years younger than me and only 13 at the time.

Geoffrey and I joined a rebellion in the South.

ive years later I gave birth to two sons in quick succession, Henry and Geoffrey. My father was delighted... but not enough to persuade the barons in Normandy to give me their allegiance, and I needed it if I were to take over my father's titles. His visits to see his grandsons were stormy and we quarrelled violently. Our relationship deteriorated to the point where Geoffrey and I joined a rebellion in the South, joining forces with Robert of Gloucester (my half-brother) to capture some key castles.

As so often happens, death and new life collided. Father had been over to visit us and it hadn't gone well. He was very upset and tucked into a huge meal of his favourite fish — lampreys — against his doctor's orders. He got food poisoning that night and died on 1 December 1135. He hadn't known I was already pregnant with my third son, whom I named for my brother, William.

A surfeit of lampreys

And so the cards were dealt. My father died without an agreed succession plan. Was it bad luck or destiny that meant we were down south near Rouen at the time? Whereas my cousin Stephen was up north in Boulogne — a mere day's journey from England. He and his army reached London by 8 December and, with his brother the Bishop of Winchester's help, persuaded the barons that Henry I had, on his death bed, changed his mind about me succeeding him.

hey didn't take much persuading. Writing off a woman's competence to rule is a well-worn path and has affected more histories than England's. Stephen and Matilda were crowned in Westminster Abbey before the year was up.

Stephen didn't have an easy time of it though. Geoffrey and I made inroads in Normandy and the Scots invaded the north of England. Revolts in South Wales, Kent and the south-west of England meant Stephen was fighting on all fronts and had to split his resources. He sent his wife to retake Dover with ships and men from Boulogne, he sent his knights to the North, and he himself went west, to regain Gloucestershire.

aking advantage of the chaos, I 'invaded' my homeland, England, in 1139. We landed at Arundel on the south coast, with 140 knights and Robert of Gloucester. I held the castle while Robert marched to Wallingford and Bristol to raise support for the rebellion. Stephen promptly marched south and besieged Arundel castle, trapping me there for a short while until he released me to join Robert in Gloucester. I will never know why he let me go. Was he confident I wasn't a threat? Was it chivalry? Was it family loyalty? Or did the burden of kingship weigh too heavy on his shoulders even then?

*We landed at Arundel on the south coast, with
140 knights and my half-brother,
Robert of Gloucester.*

hatever the reason, I established my court in Gloucester and my territory extended south into Wiltshire, west to Bristol and the Welsh Marches, and east to Wallingford, Reading and Oxford. Stephen's attention was meanwhile drawn northwards by one of my supporters, who had captured Lincoln castle.

he townspeople appealed to Stephen for help and up he marched, not realising that Robert was right behind him. It was a bloody battle, with fighting in the streets and disastrous attempted escapes by the civilians across the winter-swollen river Fossdyke. Too many lives were lost, but Stephen was captured and handed over to me. I imprisoned him in Bristol castle. I wasn't going to make the same mistake he'd made by releasing me!

LADY·OF·ENGLAND AND·NORMANDY

*After a ceremonial procession
to Winchester Cathedral, I was acclaimed
as 'Lady of England and Normandy'.*

ith Stephen imprisoned, I made preparations to take the throne. First I needed the support of the Church. Early in 1141, I met Bishop Henry and other clerics, including Abbot Edward of Reading. I had to make some concessions of course, and promise to be guided by Bishop Henry. But we made a deal and, after a ceremonial procession to Winchester Cathedral, I was acclaimed as 'Lady of England and Normandy' as a precursor to my coronation.

READING ABBEY

I stopped in Reading, where I was warmly received by many of the townspeople, and visited my father's tomb in the abbey.

y fortunes were looking up and I set out for London. I stopped over in Reading, where I was warmly received by many of the townspeople, and visited my father's tomb in the abbey. To reinforce my support, I donated some of my lands to the abbey and appointed one of the monks as Bishop of London.

Arriving in London, I met with the burghers, who were prepared to support me, but I pressed too hard on taxes, refusing to give way. Perhaps I was overconfident, too close to the culmination of my dreams to give a measured response. As my first husband learnt, rulers tread a very fine line between their friends and their foes. At the same time, Queen Matilda was petitioning me for the release of Stephen, which I also refused. This swung the Londoners against me and, along with Matilda's forces who were camped close to the city, they drove me out and I beat a hasty retreat to Oxford on 24 June.

ishop Henry changed sides (again!) to support his brother Stephen, so Robert and I besieged him in his palace at Winchester, but again, Matilda of Boulogne out-manoeuvred me. Bringing her forces up behind us, she encircled us as we encircled the palace and, while I managed to escape to Devizes, Robert was captured and our forces vanquished.

he stage was set for a prisoner swap and that's what ensued — Robert for Stephen. Clever Matilda of Boulogne! A fresh coronation of Stephen and Matilda took place in November so, a year later, with too many losses and deaths behind us, we were back to where we had started. But this time Stephen wasn't going to make the same mistake. He wanted me out of the way. He stormed Oxford, trapping me in the castle and then besieging it for three long months. Conditions were dreadful and just before Christmas, I scaled the wall on a rope and escaped across the frozen Thames. The snow camouflaged me as I walked right through Stephen's sleeping soldiers wearing white! My army surrendered the next day.

I scaled the wall on a rope and escaped across the frozen Thames wearing white camouflage.

For 11 long years we continued that civil war. Those who didn't recognise my claim to the throne called it The Anarchy. The fighting divided towns and families and even desecrated holy ground. The castle built in the grounds of Reading Abbey should never have been necessary. It was said that during that time, 'Christ and his saints slept'. I'm not proud of it. I saw it as the means to an end — a just and right 'end'. But war is rarely just and I lost sight of that. There were numerous battles, but the stalemate didn't shift. I left England in 1148 and returned to Normandy.

e finally reached a peace settlement in 1153 and that was down to Matilda of Boulogne too. She died of a fever in 1152 and was buried at Faversham Abbey. Stephen was devastated and was dealt a further blow when his son and heir, Eustace, also died. He agreed to adopt my son, Henry, as his heir. We are family, after all. Stephen died in 1154 and Henry II became King. He united vast swathes of the British Isles and France in a relatively peaceful reign. He pulled down the abominable castle at Reading Abbey. He did make the same mistake as my first husband in making an enemy of the Church, and his reputation never recovered. But that's another story...

he Empress Matilda was laid to rest in 1167 in her favourite abbey, Le Bec, in Normandy. The abbey was destroyed by the English in the 100 Years' War and her bones were lost, but they were re-discovered in the 19th century and she now lies in Rouen cathedral.

Her epitaph reads,

Ortu magna, viro maior,
sed maxima partu,
Hic iacet Henrici filia, sponsa, parens.

which means,

Great by birth, greater by marriage,
greatest in her offspring,
here lies the daughter, wife, and mother of Henry.

My son became King Henry II.

Chronology

1102 Matilda is born, probably in Winchester but possibly in Sutton (now Sutton Courtenay).

1110 Matilda becomes queen of Germany on her betrothal to Henry V, king of Germany.

1114 Matilda marries Henry V, 20 years her senior, aged 12.

1116 Henry V and Matilda march over the Alps with an army to take control of Northern Italy. Matilda stays, acting as Henry's regent.

1118 Matilda's mother, Matilda of Scotland, dies.

1120 Matilda's brother, William, heir to the English throne, dies in the White Ship disaster.

1125 Henry V dies leaving Matilda without title, home or land at the age of 23. She returns to Normandy.

1127 The English barons are persuaded to swear allegiance to Matilda as her father, Henry I's successor.

1128 Matilda marries Geoffrey of Anjou, 13 years her junior, as a strategic alliance. Later they have three sons; Henry, Geoffrey and William.

1135 Henry I, king of England, dies on 1 December without an agreed succession plan.

Stephen of Blois, Matilda's cousin, beats her in the race to seize the crown and, with the help of his wife, Matilda of Boulogne, is crowned King on 22 December.

1139 Matilda invades her homeland, England, with the help of her half-brother, Robert of Gloucester. Matilda is captured by Stephen but then released.

1141 February: Battle of Lincoln. Stephen is captured and imprisoned in Bristol castle.

April: Matilda is acclaimed 'Lady of England and Normandy' as a precursor to her coronation.

Matilda spends time in Reading on her way to London. She is welcomed by the townspeople, makes grants to the abbey and appoints one of the monks as Bishop of London.

June: Matilda's negotiations with the burghers in London go disastrously wrong, the townspeople swing against her and she has to flee back to Oxford.

July: Matilda besieges Winchester but Matilda of Boulogne encircles her forces and Robert of Gloucester is captured.

November: In an exchange of prisoners, Stephen and Robert are both released. Stephen and Matilda of Boulogne are reaffirmed as King and queen of England at Christmas.

1142 Matilda's army surrenders following the siege of Oxford although Matilda escapes to Devizes across the frozen Thames.

1148 Matilda leaves England for Normandy after Robert of Gloucester dies.

1152 Stephen's wife, Matilda of Boulogne, dies, followed by his son and heir, Eustace.

1153 A peace settlement is reached and Stephen adopts Matilda's son Henry as his heir.

1154 King Stephen dies and Henry II succeeds him as king of England in December.

1167 Matilda dies in Rouen, France.

Author's note and acknowledgements

Working with Sally Castle on this book has been a life highlight!

An enormous fan of her work, I particularly enjoyed publishing her interpretation of *The Happy Prince* by Oscar Wilde, set within the rooftops and streetscapes of Reading. When she proposed a new book on the Empress Matilda, I jumped at the opportunity to help her with the text.

We were inspired by Lindsay Mullaney's account of Matilda's life on the Reading Museum website, but needed a book-length story that would appeal to readers of 11 years and upwards. Not being a historian, I found many of the accounts of the Empress's life on the Internet confusing. The cast of characters was long and so many of them had the same names!

However, many spider diagrams and sketched-out family trees later, I was able to put together a list of 'scenes' I thought might inspire Sally and she got to work on some sketches which delighted the team – especially the butcher clinging to the rock after the White Ship disaster.

Linking these visual scenes together to form a story required some artistic licence and I developed my own view of the Empress's character derived from my reading about her mother and grandmother. I simplified the details of the Anarchy and left out some of the key protagonists to cut down on the number of characters I had to introduce.

But I was still struggling to create a sense of connection with the reader until, on the advice of my son, Arron, I rewrote the whole thing in the first person.

Proper historians will be relieved to know that this Internet-researched text has been checked by experts! I am indebted to Dr Jitske Jasperse, Assistant Professor of Medieval Visual Cultures at the Humboldt-Universität, Berlin; Danna Messer, a queenship scholar as well as Managing Editor at Arc Humanities; and Matthew Williams, Reading Museum Manager for their reviews.

We are also very grateful to Lindy Grant FSA, FRHistS, Professor Emeritus of Medieval History at the University of Reading, for her introduction.

Most of all, I'm grateful to Sally Castle for the opportunity to work with her on this, my final project with Two Rivers Press before embarking on a new career. What a wonderful way to finish!

Sally Mortimore

Illustrator's note

Sally Mortimore's idea to write the book in the first person was a great inspiration and certainly gives the story a personal feel. What a great story about an amazing woman.

My research for the illustrations for this book has been one of serendipity. I was immediately inspired by medieval manuscripts, especially the decorative illuminated letters and the simple primary colours, which gave me an idea for the overall feel of the book. Stained-glass windows inspired the style of illustration. I drew the illustrations on white scraperboard then added colour to give the bright effect of stained glass.

While researching, I found a stained-glass self-portrait by Pauline Boty. This led to my reading her biography, where she was described as 'The only blonde in a man's world'; this could also be said of Empress Matilda?

Another personal discovery was the stained-glass artwork of Scottish artist Pinkie Maclure, whose work such as Beauty Tricks references contemporary issues.

I noticed that many stained-glass windows included ornamental patterned fragments, usually in black on a colour background. The patterns reminded me of Peter Hay's rubber stamps, which were used for the earliest Two Rivers Press books and are still used sometimes. I have used some of them in the illustrations, deliberately keeping their rough stamping texture.

Each illustration led to interesting specific research; this included a stained-glass window at Winchester Cathedral. The huge west window over the cathedral entrance is not typical of an 11th-century church.

Rather than a biblical scene, it is a mosaic of fragments which had been recovered after the 1642 ransacking of the cathedral during the Civil War. Fragments from the original biblical scenes have a new spiritual message: something shattered can be put back together, maybe not as it was but still a thing of beauty? For the eagle-eyed, my illustration echoes the shape of the Winchester Cathedral window and includes fragments of other illustrations in this book.

The illuminated lettering capitals at the beginning of each page are an interpretation of original illuminated medieval lettering. They are my own loose version rather than a slavish copy. I had a bit of fun with them; in fact this whole book has been fun to do and I hope that feeling passes on to the reader.

I would like to thank all at Two Rivers Press (especially Sally M), my friends and family for their support and encouragement. I cannot end without thanking Nadja Robinson in particular for her technical help and personal patience.

Sally Castle
Sally Castle has illustrated many Two Rivers Press books, including:

Sumer is Icumen In
The Happy Prince by Oscar Wilde
Paris Scenes by Charles Baudelaire, trans. Ian Brinton
Places And Other Poems by Thomas Hardy
Believing in Reading by Adam Sowan
Bizarre Berkshire by Duncan Mackay
Reading Poetry: An anthology edited by Peter Robinson
Eat Wild by Duncan Mackay
English Nettles by Peter Robinson
Abattoirs Road to Zinzan Street by Adam Sowan

Sources and references

Empress Matilda's life story

https://www.readingmuseum.org.uk/blog/
matilda-empress-thames-valley
'Matilda – an Empress in the Thames Valley'
by Lindsay Mullaney (Reading Museum, 2018)

https://en.wikipedia.org/wiki/Empress_Matilda
Wikipedia entry for 'Empress Matilda'

Queenhithe

https://londonpavementgeology.co.uk/wp-content/
uploads/2014/11/Queenhithe.pdf
'Queenhithe' by Ruth Siddall, *Urban Geology in London* No. 8
A walk through this ancient ward of the City of London

The London Encyclopaedia by B. Weinreb et al.
(Macmillan, 2010), cited in *Urban Geology in London* No. 8

Places and people

The British Museum, The British Library, and Reading
Museum all hold collections related to Empress Matilda.

Pauline Boty: British Pop Art's sole sister
by Marc Kristal (Frances Lincoln, 2023)
A biography of this innovative woman artist and
founding member of the British Pop Art movement

https://www.pinkiemaclure.net
The website of Scottish stain-glass artist Pinkie Maclure

https://stainedglassmuseum.com
The Stained Glass Museum, Ely

Medieval style & lettering:

Bestiaire médiéval des animaux familiers
by René Cintré (Éditions Ouest-France, 2012)

Le passion du livre au Moyen Age
by S. Cassagnes-Brouquet (Éditions Ouest-France, 2012)

Masterpieces: Medieval art
by James Robinson (British Museum Press, 2012)

Alphabets and numbers of the Middle Ages
by Henry Shaw (Bracken Books, 1995)

History of Britain in maps: Over 90 maps of our nation through time
by Philip Parker (Collins, 2017)

These are only a few of many sources and references –
I was reaching for my camera in every church that
I visited!

Two Rivers Press has been publishing in and about Reading
since 1994. Founded by the artist Peter Hay (1951–2003), the press
continues to delight readers, local and further afield, with its varied list
of individually designed, thought-provoking books.